TABLE of CONTENTS

CHAPTER ONE

INTRODUCING THE BEEHIVE STATE

A runner enjoys the beautiful scenery of the Coral Pink Sand Dunes in southwestern Utah.

Utah is a place of contrasts. There are hot deserts where heat waves shimmer over the ground. There are snowy mountain peaks where the bald eagle is king. You'll also find grassy mountain meadows dotted with flowers, and glittering salt flats.

Utah was once called the State of Deseret. It was named by the area's first Caucasian settlers, the Mormons. *Deseret* is a Mormon word that means "honey bee." The bee is a symbol of hard work. The Mormons named their new homeland after the honey bee because they knew it would take hard work and cooperation to make the Salt Lake Valley a good place to live. Later, Utah was nicknamed the Beehive State because hardworking honey bees live in a beehive. If you look at Utah's state flag and seal, you will see a beehive on both of them.

When the region became a United States territory in 1850, Utah was given its present name by the United States Congress. The territory was named after the Ute, a group of Native Americans who had lived in the area for thousands of years. The word *Utah* means "people of the mountains."

You can learn even more about Utah from its state motto. Its motto is "Industry," another word that means hard work. It took the industry, teamwork, and courage of many Utahns to turn empty desert into a great place to live.

What comes to mind when you think of Utah?

- Rugged mountain men and explorers such as Jim Bridger and Jedediah Smith
- Promontory Point, where the transcontinental railroad's gold spike was laid
- The Great Salt Lake
- The headquarters of the worldwide Mormon Church
- Dinosaurs, including the deadly utahraptor
- The Utah Jazz basketball team
- World-speed records set on the Bonneville Salt Flats
- Salt Lake City, site of the 2002 Winter Olympic Games

In this book, you will discover new and interesting things about the Beehive State. Utah has a rich history, fascinating people, and exciting attractions. Turn the page and enjoy the story of Utah!

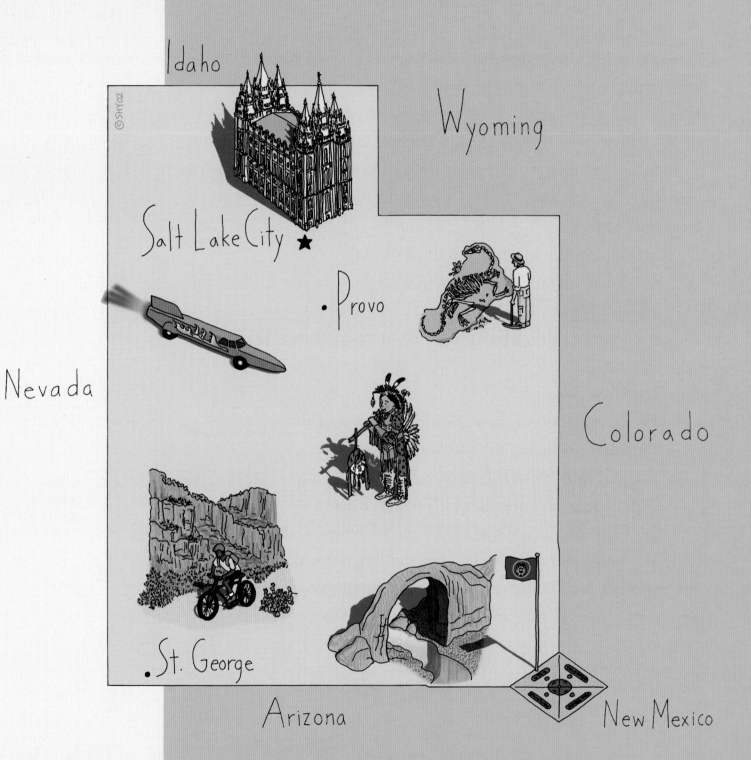

Idaho

Wyoming

Salt Lake City ★

Provo

Nevada

Colorado

St. George

Arizona

New Mexico

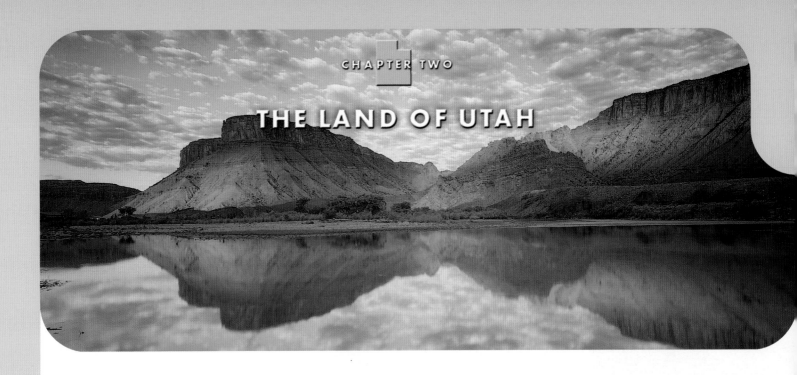

CHAPTER TWO

THE LAND OF UTAH

Utah is a Rocky Mountain state in the western United States. On a map, look for the state shaped like a long envelope standing on one end. If the "stamp" in the top right corner is torn off, you have found Utah.

Utah measures 350 miles (563 kilometers) long, and 275 miles (443 km) wide. With an area of 84,899 square miles (219,887 square kilometers), the Beehive State is the eleventh largest in the country. However, you would still need three Utahs to equal the size of Texas.

Utah is surrounded by six other states. Idaho and Wyoming are to the north, and Colorado is to the east. Arizona lies due south, and Nevada is located along Utah's western border. New Mexico, Colorado, and Arizona touch Utah's southeastern corner. The meeting point of these four states is called Four Corners Monument. It is the only place in the country where four states meet. If you kneel down on the exact

Utah's land is its most precious resource.

spot where the states touch, you can put your hands and feet in all four states at the same time.

EXTRA! EXTRA!

Have you ever left your footprint in mud or wet sand? If so, it could become a fossil. A fossil is the hardened remains of a plant or animal from long ago. It can also be the hardened impression, or print, that they leave behind. In most places, dinosaur fossils are buried deep below the ground. However, the volcanic eruptions that occurred beneath Utah many years ago pushed a layer of ancient rock up to the surface. This layer, called the Morrison Formation, contains many dinosaur fossils, making it easier to find fossils in Utah than in other places. Each year, millions of people visit Utah's Dinosaur National Monument to see the fossils.

LAND OF CONTRASTS

More than 2,500 million years ago, the climate around the world grew very warm. This change in climate melted the huge sheets of ice, called glaciers, which had covered the land. These colossal masses of ice began to slide south, like giant sleds. Mountains were crushed beneath them, and new valleys were carved out by the shifting ice.

Powerful volcanic eruptions and earthquakes also changed the land. Earthquakes opened huge cracks, or rifts, in Utah's rocky crust. Volcanic gases and lava flows pushed enormous plates of ancient rock up and over younger rock formations. The volcanic action below the

Earth's crust and the movement of glaciers created present-day Utah's three geographic regions. They are the Colorado Plateau, the Basin and Range Region, and the Rocky Mountain Region.

Colorado Plateau

Most of southeastern Utah lies in the Colorado Plateau. Within this large region are three smaller areas. They are the High Plateaus, the Canyonlands, and the Uinta Basin.

The Wasatch, Sevier, and Paunsaugunt Plateaus make up the High Plateaus, which rise along the western edge of the Colorado Plateau. These plateaus are actually *mesas*, the Spanish word for "tables." They are called mesas because they have flat tops and steep sides, like tables. The mesas measure 40 miles (64 km) across, and are more than 11,000 feet (3,353 meters) high. Together, they form an escarpment (a steep wall) that reaches south toward Arizona. The plentiful grass and water of the mesas are good for grazing livestock. In this area, sheep and goats are raised for their wool and meat.

The beautiful canyons and rock formations of the Colorado Plateau are known as the Canyonlands. Rocky arches, bridges, and rounded hills rise up in a fiery rainbow of colors. These natural sculptures are made of sandstone or limestone. They were shaped by water and wind erosion, which means that the rock was worn away by water and wind over a long period of time. The Colorado River, which flows through the eastern part of the Canyonlands, smoothed and shaped

The unusual-looking rock formations at Bryce Canyon are known as hoodoos.

this awesome scenery over thousands of years. Some of the area's most famous canyons are Bryce Canyon, Cedar Breaks Canyon, and Zion Canyon.

The plants that grow in the dry, hot climate of the Canyonlands need less than 10 inches (25 centimeters) of rain each year to survive. Among them are greasewood, creosote, and saltbush. The Canyonlands are also home to lizards and rattlesnakes.

Unlike many other plants, saltbrush can tolerate hot, dry conditions.

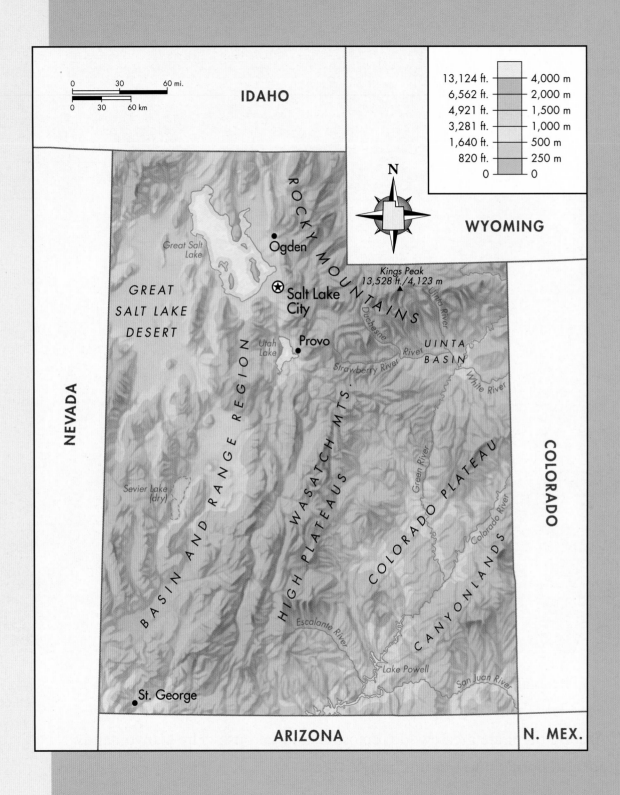

IDAHO

0   30   60 mi.
0   30   60 km

13,124 ft. — 4,000 m
6,562 ft. — 2,000 m
4,921 ft. — 1,500 m
3,281 ft. — 1,000 m
1,640 ft. — 500 m
820 ft. — 250 m
0 — 0

N

WYOMING

Great Salt Lake

● Ogden

GREAT
SALT LAKE
DESERT

☆ Salt Lake
City

Utah Lake

● Provo

Kings Peak
13,528 ft./4,123 m ▲

Duchesne River

UINTA
BASIN

Strawberry River

Uinta River

White River

ROCKY MOUNTAINS

NEVADA

BASIN AND RANGE REGION

Sevier Lake (dry)

WASATCH MTS.

HIGH PLATEAUS

Green River

COLORADO PLATEAU

Colorado River

COLORADO

CANYONLANDS

Escalante River

Lake Powell

San Juan River

● St. George

ARIZONA

N. MEX.

The Uinta Basin is a shallow, bowl-shaped area between the Book Cliffs and the Wasatch Mountains. It has an elevation of 5,000 feet (1,524 m) above sea level. Just 6 inches (15 cm) to 8-1/2 inches (22 cm) of rain fall there each year. However, several rivers and creeks drain into the Uinta Basin and keep the area from becoming too dry. Among these rivers are the Strawberry, the Green, the Duchesne, the White, and the Uinta Rivers.

Many dinosaur fossils have been found in the Uinta Basin's Morrison Formation. Not all of Utah's rock contains dinosaur fossils, however. Some layers contain precious metals such as gold, silver, and copper. Others contain important natural resources like oil, gas, radium, uranium, and coal, the state rock. Mining these natural resources has added millions of dollars to Utah's economy.

The Basin and Range Region

The Basin and Range Region covers the western part of Utah. Like the Uinta Basin, the elevation of the Basin is lower than the land all around it, like a huge empty bowl. However, this "bowl" was not always empty. It once held a giant lake that scientists named Lake Bonneville. This ancient lake had an area of 20,000 square miles (51,799 sq km).

As the world's climate became warmer, the water in Lake Bonneville evaporated, or dried up. Today, the Bonneville Salt Flats are 30,000 acres (12,141 hectares) of hardened salt crystals that were left behind when Lake Bonneville dried up. These dazzling white stretches are now used as a racetrack, where many world-speed records have been set.

A race car speeds down the Bonneville Salt Flats.

Rocky Mountain Region

Two mountain ranges enter Utah at its northeastern corner. They are the Wasatch Range and the Uinta Range. These ranges are both part of the enormous Rocky Mountain Range that runs north to south through the United States. Both ranges contain gold, silver, and copper ores.

One of the world's largest open-pit copper mines is Utah's Bingham Copper Mine in the Oquirrh Mountains. Bingham has been mined continuously since 1863. The mine's open pit is 2-1/2 miles (4 km) across and 1/2 mile (0.8 km) deep. Over the years, more than 5 billion tons (4.5 billion metric tons) of dirt, 14-1/2 million tons (13 million metric tons) of copper, 620 tons (562 metric tons) of gold, and 5,000 tons (4,535 metric tons) of silver have been trucked out of it. The pit, or hole, left behind is so big that it can be seen from space shuttles orbiting Earth!

The Wasatch Range reaches from Mount Nebo in north central Utah, to the Idaho border. The Wasatch Range's elevation averages 10,000 feet (3,048 m) above sea level. Like most mountain ranges in the United States, the Wasatch Range runs from north to south.

The Uinta Range begins in neighboring Colorado and runs 150 miles (241 km) to Salt Lake City, in north central Utah. Many peaks in

The Bingham Copper Mine is so large that the Sears Tower, one of the tallest buildings in the world, would only reach halfway up the side of the pit.

this range reach more than 13,000 feet (3,962 m), including Kings Peak, which rises 13,528 feet (4,123 m). Kings Peak is Utah's highest point. At this elevation, there are mountain meadows and forests of pine, spruce, and juniper trees. The wilderness is home to cougars, bobcats, mule-deer, foxes, and other animals.

RIVERS AND LAKES

The Colorado River is one of the longest rivers in the United States. It begins in western Colorado, then flows southeast through Utah and the Grand Canyon, until it reaches the Gulf of California. A major tributary of the Colorado River is the Green River, which flows south from Wyoming and joins the Colorado River in the canyon country of southeast Utah. The water from these two rivers generates hydroelectric

The Colorado River is one of the great rivers of North America.

power for people who live in cities along the Wasatch Front. Hydroelectric power is produced by the force of moving water.

Another tributary of the Colorado is the San Juan River. The smaller Provo, Weber, and Bear Rivers begin in the Wasatch and Uinta mountain ranges. Utah's Escalante River, named after Franciscan explorer Silvestre Vélez de Escalante, was the last major river to be discovered in the United States.

Utah's largest lake is Great Salt Lake, located in the north central part of Utah's Basin and Range region. It has an area of 4,080 square miles (10,567 sq km), making it the largest saltwater lake in all of North America. The lake's average depth is 30 feet (9 m), but the water level changes during the summer because of evaporation.

Great Salt Lake got its name because it is one-quarter salt (two to three times saltier than seawater). However, Great Salt Lake is only the

Small islands, called islets, on Great Salt Lake provide nesting places for seagulls, terns, and blue herons.

FIND OUT MORE

People and objects float more easily in salt water than in plain water. Can you think of a simple experiment to prove that this is true?

EXTRA! EXTRA!

Although it is 500 miles (804 km) from the nearest ocean, Great Salt Lake smells fishy—like the seashore. What's the reason for that fishy smell? It comes from the lake's "sandy" beaches, which are not sand at all. They are made of the gritty waste of millions of brine shrimp!

second saltiest lake in the world. The highest levels of salt are found in Israel's Dead Sea, where the water is seven times saltier than seawater.

The first Mormon settlers used salt from Great Salt Lake to keep their food from spoiling. Every year, tons of salt is taken from the lake to use in homes and businesses all over the United States. The salt you sprinkle on your popcorn may come from Utah's Great Salt Lake. Although you can eat the salt from the lake, tiny brine shrimp are the only creatures that can live in such salty water. Utah's state bird, the California seagull, thrives on these shrimp.

Next in size is Utah Lake, the state's largest freshwater lake. Utah Lake empties into Great Salt Lake. It is 8 miles (13 km) wide and 23 miles (37 km) long, and has an area of 150 square miles (388 sq km).

Lake Powell, south of the Basin and Range region, has more than 2,000 miles (3,219 km) of shoreline. It is the second largest man-made lake in the world. This popular recreation spot attracts more than 3 million boaters, campers, and hikers each year.

Lake Powell was made by building Glen Canyon Dam in neighboring Arizona. This enormous dam is part of the Colorado River Storage Project. More than 15 million gallons (56,793,531 liters) of water pass through the watergates of the

Glen Canyon Dam each minute. The hydroelectricity that is generated by this water supplies power for 1-1/2 million people in Utah, Arizona, Wyoming, California, and Colorado.

A breathtaking red bridge of natural stone called Rainbow Bridge rises from the shores of Lake Powell. Rainbow Bridge is 290 feet (88.4 m) tall and spans 275 feet (84 m) across the Colorado River. It is sacred to the Navajo people.

Rainbow Bridge is one of the world's largest natural bridges.

Many skiers agree that Utah has the greatest snow on earth.

CLIMATE

Utah is sunny for about 237 days each year. Its hottest month is July, when the state's average summer temperature rises to a sizzling 93.2° Fahrenheit (34° Celsius). (Although this temperature is the average, many areas will have higher temperatures—and others lower—depending on their elevation and location in Utah.) The record high temperature is 117°F (47°C). It was recorded on July 5, 1985, at St. George in southwestern Utah.

In January, Utah's average temperature drops to a wintry 19°F (–7°C). The lowest temperature on record is –69°F (–56°C). It was recorded on February 1, 1985, at Peter's Sink, which rises 8,092 feet (2,466 m) above sea level.

Precipitation, or moisture, varies widely across Utah's three geographic regions. The state's average rainfall is 16 inches (41 cm). However, in the dry, hot deserts of Utah's Basin and Range Region, as little as 5 inches (12.7 cm) of rain falls each year. The Rocky Mountain Range gets a soaking with 60 inches (152 cm) of rain, and the Wasatch Range has more than 60 inches (152 cm) of dry, powdery snow each winter.

Two or three tornadoes touch down in Utah each year. Tornadoes occur during thunderstorms, when warm, damp air rises, crashing into the cooler air above it. A powerful wind spins this air around. This spinning action creates the tornado's powerful funnel, or spinning column of air. On August 11, 1999, a low-grade F2 tornado tore up Salt Lake City. Its winds were between 113 mph (181 kph) and 157 mph (253 kph). This twister killed one person and injured 50 others. It also caused $100 million in property damage.

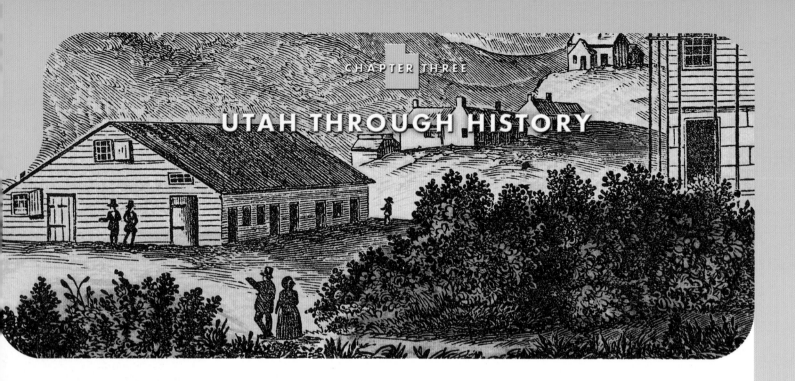

CHAPTER THREE

UTAH THROUGH HISTORY

This drawing shows a view of Salt Lake City around 1859. Brigham Young's home is shown on the right.

About 450 million years ago, the land we call Utah was covered by leafy forests. These forests were home to plant-eating dinosaurs such as the stegosaurus, the utahraptor, and the allosaurus. Many years later, these dinosaurs died out. Their skeletons hardened between layers of earth and became fossils.

The first human beings in Utah were called Paleo-Indians. They lived in Utah 11,000 years ago. They lived close to lakes and marshes, where there was fresh water to drink. They gathered wild plants and berries in the forests, or caught fish from the rivers. They also hunted small animals such as rabbits and antelopes.

EXTRA! EXTRA!

The first utahraptor fossils were discovered in 1981 by paleontologists, scientists who study plant and animal remains from long ago. The utahraptor was 20 feet (6 m) long and weighed just under 1 ton. Its front and back legs ended in 10-inch (25-cm) and 15-inch (38-cm) claws. When the utahraptor kicked out, it slashed a deadly wound in its prey. Even so, the utahraptor hunted in gangs because it was smaller than most of its meat-eating cousins.

Some Paleo-Indians were hunter-gatherers. They moved from place to place, following herds of bison and woolly mammoths. They hunted these large prehistoric animals using arrows and spears tipped with obsidian, a black rock that is found in Utah's Great Basin Region. Paleo-Indians traded arrowheads and pottery with people in the southwest.

About 9,000 years ago, the world's climate became hotter and drier. As temperatures rose, the lakes dried up, and the leafy forests and grassy meadows became empty deserts. The herds of woolly mammoth and bison died out because their grazing land was gone. In order to survive, Paleo-Indians became farmers instead of hunters, and planted maize, beans, and squash.

Paleo-Indians were the ancestors of Utah's prehistoric Native American groups. Among these groups were the Fremont band, who were hunters of the Uinta Basin's desert regions, and the Anasazi. Traces of Fremont and Anasazi villages have been found all around Utah by anthropologists (scientists who study ancient peoples).

Anasazi pottery, shown here, is preserved and studied in an effort to learn more about the Ancient Ones.

THE ANCIENT ONES

The Anasazi, or "Ancient Ones," were farmers who lived in the Four Corners area of Utah from about 100 B.C. to A.D. 1300. They lived in homes made of adobe, or mud, tucked high in the canyon walls. The Anasazi stayed in one place, gathering pine nuts and planting crops such as maize, squash, and beans. They stored rice, seed-corn, and pine nuts

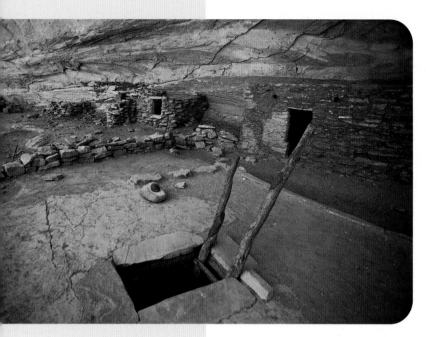

You can see the remains of an Anasazi kiva in Grand Gulch.

in coiled clay pots. These pots were decorated with beautiful designs such as triangles, circles, or spirals. The designs showed important events in the Anasazi's lives.

The Anasazi people worshipped nature gods, such as the sun and the rain. The men held ceremonies to honor these gods in a sacred room called the kiva or "place of worship." The priests of the Anasazi religion were called kachina. For special ceremonies, the kachina danced sacred dances dressed in animal costumes. They also used kachina dolls, dressed with bits of fur and buckskin, to teach Anasazi children about the kachina spirits of nature. The spirits brought rain, sun, and food to the Anasazi people.

Around A.D. 1300 or A.D. 1400, the Anasazi disappeared from the Colorado Plateau. Anthropologists do not know why the Anasazi left Utah, or where they went. Some believe the climate became too hot and dry to grow crops. Others think they traveled southwest to join the Pueblo people.

NATIVE AMERICANS OF UTAH

After the Anasazi vanished, several Native American tribes made Utah their home. Among them were the Ute, Goshute, Shoshone, Hopi, Navajo, and Paiute.

The lands of the Ute people once stretched from Denver, Colorado, to the Salt Lake Desert, and down to the pueblos, or towns, of New Mexico. The Ute were the first Native Americans to trade for horses with the Spanish in New Mexico. Horses quickly became very important to the Ute. They followed the buffalo herds and hunted on horseback. When the tribe moved, they took their tepees, or homes, with them.

The early Ute hunted antelope on the Utah plains.

Tepees were made by Ute women. The women scraped several buffalo hides, or skins, with a special tool called a flesher to remove scraps of fat and skin. When the skins were clean, they were sewn together, then stretched over a frame of straight wooden poles, like a tent. The Ute people also built shelters made of branches, called wickiups. These shelters were cool in hot summer months.

The Ute believed in the supernatural world of ghosts and spirits. The shaman, or medicine man, was believed to have special powers. He used his powers, chants, and sacred eagle-feathers to heal the sick. The Ute also believed in gods of nature. The most important Ute rituals were the Bear Dance and the Sun Dance. At these ceremonies, they asked the Creator to give their people power and strength.

The Goshute people inhabited the harsh deserts of western Utah. They were hunter-gatherers who lived in family groups. These groups

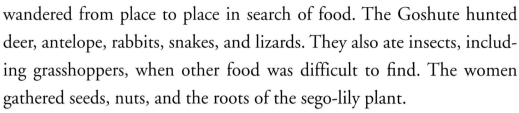

wandered from place to place in search of food. The Goshute hunted deer, antelope, rabbits, snakes, and lizards. They also ate insects, including grasshoppers, when other food was difficult to find. The women gathered seeds, nuts, and the roots of the sego-lily plant.

The Southern Paiute people lived in the southwestern region of Utah. They hunted on foot, and planted gardens of corn and beans in the floodplains of the rivers. Although they were a peace-loving people, Paiute villages were often raided by the Ute. Paiute women and children were sometimes taken captive and sold as slaves in New Mexico.

The Navajo People called themselves the Diné, or The People. The Spanish word *navajo* means "people who have land." The first Diné came to Utah around A.D. 1300. They settled in the area that is now called Four Corners. Like the Ute, the Diné were hunter-gatherers. They kept herds of goats and sheep, planted crops, and wove beautiful blankets. Navajo families lived in traditional homes called hogans.

Like their name (which means the "peaceful people"), the Hopi were a peaceful tribe, unlike their Ute neighbors. The Hopi lived in one- or two-story adobe houses that were grouped together in pueblos, towns, or cities. They were primarily farmers who grew cotton, maize, beans, and squash.

A Navajo family stands outside their hogan, made from a framework of logs covered with earth.

EUROPEAN EXPLORATION

Between 1500 and 1800, several European countries tried to claim the rich lands of North America for themselves. They hoped to mine its mountains for gold, silver, and other precious metals. One of these countries was Spain.

The first known Spanish explorer to visit present-day Utah was Juan Maria Antonio de Rivera. In 1765, the Governor of Mexico sent Rivera north to explore the northeastern part of Utah. The governor wanted Rivera to claim new lands for Spain. Rivera followed the Rio del Tizon, or the Colorado River, as far as present-day Moab. Before turning back, he found a safe place to cross the dangerous Colorado River. It is the only safe crossing in Utah.

In 1776, Spanish missionaries (priests) Father Silvestre Vélez de Escalante and Father Francisco Atanasio Dominguez came to the Utah area and kept a diary of their journey. Escalante hoped to bring the word of God to the Native Americans of Utah. He also wanted to find a safe trail through the Wasatch Mountains to the Spanish missions, or churches, along the California coast. Escalante's expedition explored the Uinta Basin and the Utah Lake area. However, blizzards forced the priests to return to New Mexico in 1777.

A Spanish expedition makes its way across the southwest.

HARDY MOUNTAIN MEN

By 1780, several European explorers had visited Utah but none settled in the area. The first Europeans to make Utah their home were fur trappers, or "mountain men." In the 1800s, fashionable winter clothes were often made from the skins of beaver and other furry animals. Animal furs (also called pelts or skins) were expensive because they were difficult to get. The business of trapping animals and selling their pelts was called the fur trade.

Hardy mountain men stayed in the mountains all year round, living off the land. They survived Utah's bitterly cold winters by hunting, fishing, and trapping. They also made friends with Native Americans. The mountain men learned to speak their language, and learned how to "track," or follow, even the smallest signs left behind by people or animals. As they explored Utah's forests, rivers, and canyons, mountain men found places where beaver, fox, and other fur-bearing animals were plentiful. They also discovered new trails, passes, and freshwater springs. Their important discoveries helped the settlers who came after them. One of the best-known mountain men was Etienne Provost, a French-Canadian. Several places in Utah are named after Provost, including Utah's second largest city, Provo.

Traders loaded furs on small boats and transported them down the Bear River.

In 1824, a Missouri businessman named William H. Ashley hired trappers to work for his new fur-trading company, which was based in St. Louis, Missouri. Ashley sent trappers to the mountains of Utah. Each spring, he collected the furs from the mountain men at their spring rendezvous, or meeting place, on Utah's Green River. Among these men were Jim Bridger, Jedediah Smith, and Miles Goodyear.

Jim Bridger was one of the first Caucasians to see the Great Salt Lake in 1824. Jedediah Smith discovered South Pass, a path through the Rocky Mountains to new territories in the west. Miles Goodyear blazed a new trail from Salt Lake City to Los Angeles, California. In the early 1840s, he built the first fort in Utah, called Fort Buenaventura, on the Weber River, where the city of Ogden now stands. In 1832, a Frenchman named Antoine Robidoux opened a small trading post in the Uinta Basin. A trading post was a store where people could trade animal furs for iron cooking pots, blankets, tobacco, rifles, and hunting knives.

During the mid-1800s, John C. Fremont, an Army engineer, explored Utah several times. He left written records of the people, animals, and plants he saw along the way. Later pioneers used the maps and diaries of Fremont and other explorers to find the safest, fastest trails across Utah.

John C. Fremont explored Utah and other parts of the southwest.

Although several people explored Utah, most of them thought that the region was too remote, or cut off from the rest of the country. One group of people, however, thought that Utah was the perfect place to live. They were the Mormons.

Mormons are members of a religious group called the Church of Jesus Christ of Latter-Day Saints (LDS). The first LDS church was started in Fayette, New York, in 1830 by Joseph Smith. In the 1840s, the LDS church began practicing polygamy, which meant that men could be married to more than one woman at a time. However, this belief clashed with the laws of the United States, which said that polygamy was illegal. The Mormons were disliked by people of other religions because of this practice. They were often persecuted, or treated cruelly, by non-Mormons. To escape persecution, 148 Mormon pioneers headed west to Missouri in wagon trains.

They didn't stay long. In 1839, Missouri governor Lilburn W. Boggs ordered the Mormons to leave. The terrified Mormons fled to Illinois. Unfortunately, the people were no different there—200 Mormon farms were burned and several Mormons were killed by people who did not agree with LDS teachings. In June 1844, Joseph Smith and his brother Hyrum were murdered by an angry mob.

The leaders of the LDS church decided it was time to find a new homeland where Mormons could live and

Joseph Smith preaches to his followers as they search for a place to settle.

worship without fear. They studied maps, hoping to find a place that nobody else wanted. When they saw a map of Utah, drawn by John C. Fremont, they knew they had found their Zion, or "heaven on earth."

Less than two years later, a wagon train carrying the first 148 Mormon pioneers left Omaha, Nebraska. They were led by their new church president, Brigham Young, another church leader, Wilford Woodruff, and others. Of the first pioneers, 140 were men of European descent, and three were African-American. There were only three women and two children in the party. On July 24, 1847, after traveling for 1,500 miles (2,414 km), the Mormon pioneers reached north central Utah. The wagon train stopped in a canyon east of present-day Salt Lake City. The settlers named the place "Emigration Canyon."

The Salt Lake Valley spread out beneath the beautiful Wasatch Mountains. There was enough vegetation for their livestock to eat. There were creeks and streams that could be channeled into ditches to water their crops. With hard work, the valley would provide everything they needed to live.

Mormons endured difficult conditions while making their way to Salt Lake City.

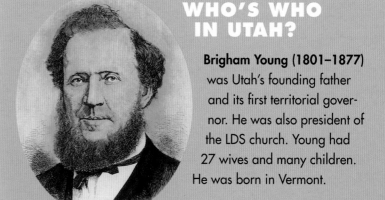

WHO'S WHO IN UTAH?

Brigham Young (1801–1877) was Utah's founding father and its first territorial governor. He was also president of the LDS church. Young had 27 wives and many children. He was born in Vermont.

EXTRA! EXTRA!

Pioneer Day, celebrated on July 24th, is a state holiday in Utah. It kicks off the state's Days of '47 celebration, held in honor of the first Mormons' arrival in the Salt Lake Valley. The celebrations last all month, with pageants, rodeos, and parades.

The settlers began plowing their fields that same day. The women and children followed the plows. They dropped seed potatoes into furrows in the sandy soil, and covered them with earth. In the days that followed, the Mormons dug ditches to change the path of the creeks. This method of watering crops is called irrigation. Within weeks, the first green shoots had sprouted.

Some of the men went into the mountains to cut down trees for timber. Others built corrals for the livestock, or made bricks of adobe. They built shelters for church services and classrooms. They also marked off the wide streets of their first town, which they named Great Salt Lake City (the "Great" was dropped in 1868). Each family was given land to build a house, plant vegetables, and keep pigs and chickens.

The Mormons called their new homeland the state of Deseret (*deseret* is a Mormon word that means "honey bee"). Like honey bees, the new settlers worked hard and prospered. By winter, another 1,650 Mormons joined the first 148 pioneers. Whenever a new wagon train

New caravans continued to arrive in Utah, bringing more settlers to develop the area.

arrived, everyone gathered together to celebrate. They danced and sang to the lively music of pianos and fiddles that were carried across the Rockies in wagons.

Although the valley held great promise, no amount of hard work stopped the settlers from worrying about their food supply. The Goshute, a Native American group living in the Salt Lake Valley, taught the Mormons how to harvest the sego lily when food was hard to find. Nevertheless, the settlers feared that there would not be enough food to last all winter. If anything happened to their crops, they would starve.

In the spring of 1848, their worst fears came true. Swarms of large, black crickets came down the mountainsides and into the Salt Lake Valley. The Mormons watched in horror as the crickets devoured their harvest. Then, out of nowhere, flocks of California seagulls swooped down and gobbled up all the crickets. The Mormons gave thanks to God and to the hungry gulls for saving their crops. The California seagull is now the state bird of Utah.

FIND OUT MORE

Are all bees busy? Worker bees certainly are. There are 20,000 worker bees in an average beehive. Their job is to gather the nectar from flowers and turn it into honey. They also care for the queen bee and clean the hive. What is the job of the queen bee?

The statue of the Miracle of the Gulls stands in Salt Lake City's Temple Square.

With the help of the Goshute, the Mormon pioneers survived their first winter. By 1853, just six years later, there were more than 16,000 Mormon settlers in Utah.

SETTLEMENT AND STATEHOOD

In 1846, Utah still belonged to Mexico. When the Mexican-American War ended in 1848, present-day Utah and other territories were handed over to the United States under the Treaty of Guadalupe Hidalgo.

Just three years after finding their new homeland, the Mormons petitioned the United States government to admit Deseret as a state. The Mormons wanted statehood so they could send representatives to Congress, the lawmaking body of the United States. With someone to represent them, they would have a voice in the government.

Deseret's request was turned down. Instead, under the Compromise of 1850, Congress created a United States territory and renamed the area Utah. The territory's borders were also changed, making Utah much smaller than it was before.

Several years later, United States President James Buchanan decided that the LDS church had too much control in Utah. He also believed that, because the Mormons continued to practice polygamy, they did not respect the government's authority. In many ways, this was true. Brigham Young ran the LDS church. He also ran the territory's government. Most of the schools, industries, and farms were owned and run by Mormons. In fact, 9 of every 10 people in Utah were Mormon.

President James Buchanan pressured the Mormons to obey United States laws.

Over the next ten years, however, English, Irish, Italians, Japanese, Chinese, Greeks, and African Americans swelled Utah's population to more than 40,000. Jews, Catholics, and Presbyterians flooded into the region. The newcomers brought with them a rich variety of cultures, religious beliefs, and customs. However, they had very little say in Utah's government because they were outnumbered by the Mormons.

In 1857, President Buchanan removed Brigham Young from office and replaced him with Governor Alfred Cumming, a non-Mormon. The president believed a non-Mormon governor would weaken the Mormons' power. His decision further heightened the tensions in Utah between Mormons and the United States government.

In the middle of this unrest, tragedy struck at Mountain Meadows in southern Utah. On September 11, 1857, a group of Mormons dressed as Native Americans attacked a party of about 140 travelers in the Utah Territory. All 136 men, women, and children were killed. Two Mormon church leaders were arrested for the murders. One of the men, John Lee, claimed that the pioneers planned to attack Mormon

WHAT'S IN A NAME?

The names of many places in Utah have interesting origins.

Name	Comes From or Means
Utah	Named after the Ute; it is a Navajo word that means "people of the mountains"
Deseret	Mormon word meaning "honey bee"
Ogden	Named for fur-trapper Peter Skene Ogden
Provo	Named for fur-trapper Etienne Provost
Wasatch	A Ute word that means "mountain pass"

The Mormons' distrust of outsiders led in part to the tragedy at Mountain Meadows, where more than 135 people were killed.

settlements. Others said that the wagon train was just passing through Utah on its way west. There were rumors that Mormon leaders had known about the attack.

President Buchanan sent the Utah Expeditionary Force to Salt Lake City to keep the peace. When they arrived, Salt Lake City was deserted. The Mormons had abandoned their city. The two sides later came to an agreement, and the Mormons allowed the Utah Expeditionary Force to stay in the Utah Territory. Over the next thirty years, Utah's leaders continued to petition for statehood without success. The government's message was clear—Utah would not be allowed to join the Union until the Mormons ended polygamy.

The settlers quarried stone for the Mormon Temple.

MAKING PROGRESS

Despite this setback, progress in other areas continued. Wide streets were laid out in Salt Lake City. A beautiful new Mormon Temple was built in the central square, using blocks of Utah granite. Churches of other faiths also sprang up, including the Roman Catholic Cathedral of the Madeleine, with its graceful spires and colorful stained-glass windows. Brigham Young's homes, the Lion House and the adobe Beehive House, were also built.

Utah's first factory, the Provo Woolen Mill, was started in 1872. Other factories, mills, businesses, and farms followed. Towns such as Provo, Ogden, Bountiful, Tooele, and Farmington sprang up along the Wasatch Front to house workers and their families.

Coal-miners came to the territory from Cornwall, Wales, and eastern Europe. They and their families added to the territory's non-Mormon population. Coal was soon being mined at Castlegate, Winter Quarters, and Clear Creek. Other mines yielded precious metals, such as gold, silver, and copper. Mining and smelting (the processing of these ores) became a profitable business for Utah.

The railroad brought people from many backgrounds to Utah, where they mined for gold, copper, and other resources.

Communication was improving rapidly, too. In 1860, the Pony Express began carrying mail between Sacramento, California, across Utah to St. Joseph, Missouri. The young men rode relays of fast ponies from place to place, and guarded the mailbag with their lives. In 1861, the Pony Express was replaced by the transcontinental telegraph. The overland telegraph made it possible for telegraphers to send news and messages from Nebraska to California in just moments. Soon, the keys of the telegraph were clicking news of the outside world to Utah's towns and outlying settlements.

A crowd of onlookers celebrated the completion of the first transcontinental railroad.

However, it was the coming of the transcontinental (cross-country) railroad that opened Utah to the rest of the country. In 1868, the Union Pacific railroad crews laid the last few rails of the transcontinental railroad through Utah's Weber and Echo Canyons. On May 10, 1869, the last spike—a golden spike—was hammered home near Promontory Point. Locomotive whistles blew and the crowds went wild! The country was now linked by rail from east to west. Journeys that once took several months by wagon now took only days by train. Goods that had been transported by wagon over rough trails were loaded onto the railroad's freight cars and carried all over the country. It was one of the most exciting moments in United States history. The railroad and the telegraph brought new people, new ideas, and new inventions flooding into Utah.

THE TERRIBLE PRICE OF PROGRESS

Between 1853 and 1890, Utah's population grew from 16,000 to more than 200,000. Most of the newcomers were Caucasians. They lived and worked in towns along the Wasatch Front, where Utah's newest industries and factories were being built.

Progress was not welcomed by everyone. As the settlers' homes, farms, and industries took over, Native Americans had to move their villages away from areas of fertile land and good hunting. The Navajo tried to resist, but in 1864, the federal government forced them to surrender their lands. The Navajo were forcibly marched to Fort Sumner, also known as Bosque Redondo, in New Mexico. This terrible journey was known as the Long Walk. It would be many years before the Navajo returned to Utah.

The Navajo were not the only Native Americans who lost their land. The settlers also forced out the Ute, leaving them with land that was too poor to produce food. The animals that the Ute had once hunted were gone. By 1868, the Ute were homeless, and many were also starving.

In 1850, the federal government opened the Indian Bureau in Washington, D.C. Indian Agencies were started in the Utah Territory. These agencies were responsible for keeping the Indian Bureau informed about what the tribes needed. The government promised to help by sending food supplies, but it was already too late. Desperate Native Americans raided Mormon farms, killing settlers and stealing their cattle for food. Church leaders ordered

The United States government encouraged Native Americans to become "westernized," so that they looked more like Europeans.

the Mormons not to fight back, but their efforts to defend themselves led to the Walker War (1853–1854) and the Black Hawk War (1865–1868). Both wars ended with many deaths on each side.

After the Black Hawk War, the Mormons asked the government to order Native Americans to leave the territory. Federal troops forced the White River, Uncompahgre, and Uintah Utes to go to the Uintah-Ouray Reservation. (A reservation is land set aside for Native Americans.) Other Ute bands were forced onto the Uintah Reservation, or sent to reservations in Colorado. The vast tribal lands of the Ute and the Navajo were lost. The lives of these proud Native Americans would never be the same again.

STATEHOOD

Despite amazing progress in transportation, communication, and industry, Utah was not yet a state. In 1877, Brigham Young died and Mormon leader Wilford Woodruff took Young's place as LDS church president.

In 1882, the federal government passed a law called the Edmunds Act. It stated that Mormon men with more than one wife would be sent to prison. Mormons who disobeyed the law could not vote or serve on juries. They would also be fired from their government jobs.

Thousands of angry Mormons left the Utah Territory because of the Edmonds Bill. Some families hid in the hills. Others fled south to Mexico with their families. Government soldiers were everywhere. It was a frightening time for the Mormon people. However, there was worse to come.

In 1887, the Edmunds-Tucker Act was passed. This act took away two things that were important to the Mormons: church funds (monies) and women's suffrage (women's right to vote). At the time, women in the United States could not vote. However, Utah law had allowed Mormon women to do so, until the passing of the Edmunds-Tucker Act.

In September 1890, Wilford Woodruff made an unexpected manifesto, or announcement. Woodruff told the Mormons that he had a vision, or religious dream. In this vision, God told him to outlaw polygamy. Woodruff told church members that they should obey the laws of the United States. Woodruff's message shocked LDS church members around the world. From that day on, polygamy was banned by the Mormon church.

Six years later, President Grover Cleveland accepted Utah's petition for statehood. In 1895, a new state constitution, or list of rules by which a state is governed, was adopted. On January 4, 1896, Utah was admitted to the Union as the forty-fifth state. The Beehive State's struggle for statehood was finally over.

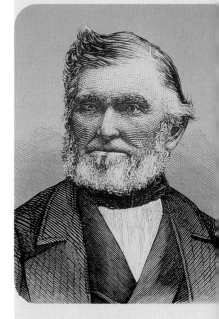

Mormon leader Wilford Woodruff shocked the church by ending polygamy.

BROKEN PROMISES

Sadly, nothing had changed for Utah's Native Americans. In 1905, the Ute lost their homes a second time, when the government gave Ute reservation lands to greedy settlers for development. Once again, the government had betrayed the Native Americans.

In 1906, the Ute left Utah. They traveled to South Dakota to join the Sioux tribes. Together, as a great army of Native Americans, they planned to rise up and take back their tribal lands. Their plan failed, however. Like the Ute, the Sioux were too poor and hungry to fight. Two years later, the federal government forced the Ute to return to their reservation under armed guard.

WORLD WAR I

During World War I (1914–1918), the countries of Great Britain, France, Belgium, Italy, and others fought against Germany and Austria-Hungary. The United States did not join this war until 1917, after the passenger ship *Lusitania* was sunk by German forces. More than 120 Americans were killed on board the ship.

Utah's Fort Douglas, founded by Captain Patrick Connor in 1862, became an important military installation during the war. The fort in Salt Lake City was used for training recruits and holding prisoners-of-war.

For several years after World War I, Utah's economy continued to grow. However, in the early 1930s, there was an economic slowdown called the Great Depression. An economic depression occurs when prices drop too low. Businesses lose so much money they cannot afford to stay open. When this happens, the people who work for these businesses lose their jobs. Banks close, and people lose their savings. On

October 29, 1929, the stock market crashed. People who had invested their money in stocks lost everything.

During the Great Depression, every state suffered hardships. One person in every four was out of work. The situation was even worse in Utah, where four of every ten people were unemployed. Unemployment among Utah's minorities was even higher during this time. Five of every ten African-Americans were unemployed during the Great Depression.

President Franklin D. Roosevelt helped the country get back on its feet by creating jobs. The government employed people to build roads and schools. However, recovery was slow and difficult. Utah's economy improved little until the outbreak of World War II.

President Roosevelt helped to end the Great Depression by giving people jobs in public works.

WORLD WAR II

On December 7, 1941, Japanese bombers attacked the U.S. Pacific Fleet at Pearl Harbor, in the United States territory of Hawaii. More than 2,500 people were killed. This attack pulled the United States into World War II (1939–1945).

Navajo code talkers sent military messages that the enemy could not decipher.

During World War II, members of Utah's Navajo Nation joined the U.S. Marines. They served their country as "Code Talkers." The Japanese were unable to break codes that were transmitted in the Navajo language, which was extremely difficult to learn. Using the code, United States officials could communicate orders that the enemy would not understand. The code helped the United States and our allies to win World War II.

With the United States at war, the demand for Utah's natural resources increased. High demand for coal, steel, and copper boosted the production of mining products. The production of farm produce, grain, and other food products was also high because hungry troops had to be fed. Missile, or weapon, plants were built in Ogden, Brigham City, and Salt Lake City. These plants provided many new jobs for the state. During the war, Utah also became an important transportation center for the United States military, because its safe inland location made it difficult to attack.

After the war, the military presence in Utah grew even larger. By 1945, there were 14 military installations in Utah. More than 62,000 Utahns were on active military duty at this time. Hill Field Air Force Base alone employed over 15,000 civilians. Defense spending became the largest contributor to Utah's economy.

In the years following World War II, the state's income from farming and ranching dropped off. However, the 1952 discovery of uranium, oil, and gas fields near Moab brought new industrial growth to the state's economy. Uranium was used to make nuclear weapons. Mining and the manufacture of steel products also increased.

In 1963, Flaming Gorge Dam on the Green River and Glen Canyon Dam on the Colorado River were completed. These dams, which are part of the Colorado River Storage Project, generate millions of kilowatts of hydroelectric power for Utah and neighboring states.

In May 1996, Utah governor Mike Leavitt created the Open Lands committee. This committee works to protect Utah's wilderness, wildlife, and environment. "There is only one chance to protect open space," Governor Leavitt said. "When it's gone, it's gone." Sadly, just four years later more than 272,000 acres (110,074 ha) of wildland were destroyed by forest fires. Governor Leavitt asked the federal government to help Utah fight the fires that were blazing out of control and destroying the wilderness.

Vast quantities of uranium were found near Moab in 1952. At the time, uranium, which was used for nuclear weapons, was more valuable than gold.

A TIME OF CELEBRATION

In 1996, Utah celebrated its 100th anniversary of statehood with parades, balls, and other festivities. At the same time, preparation

A Native American dancer performs for the German Olympic team during the 2002 Winter Olympics.

began for another exciting event—the 2002 Winter Olympic Games. In 1995, the International Olympic Committee had selected Salt Lake City to host this very important event.

The games' motto was, "The World Is Welcome Here." By February 2002, the Beehive State was ready to welcome the champion athletes and millions of fans who flocked to Salt Lake City from all over the world. At the opening ceremonies, a golden eagle, the Native American symbol of life and the spirit, soared over the watching crowds. Afterward, a traditional Native American blessing was given to the athletes by each of Utah's Native American tribes. Ghostly animal puppets, representing the state's vanishing wildlife, and pioneer wagons circled the arena. It was a breathtaking pageant of Utah's history that was seen by millions. The world was welcomed to Utah that winter. In 2002, Utah was finally welcomed to the world.

CHAPTER FOUR

GOVERNING UTAH

Utah is governed according to its constitution. A constitution contains the state's rules and laws, and defines how the state will be organized. Utah's constitution was adopted at a constitutional convention in 1895, one year before Utah became a state. The constitution divides Utah's state government into three branches, or parts: the executive branch, the legislative branch, and the judicial branch.

The Utah state capitol was completed in 1915.

EXECUTIVE BRANCH

The executive branch makes sure that the state's laws are carried out. The governor is head of the executive branch. He or she is elected by the people of Utah to serve a four-year term. The governor is assisted by a lieutenant governor. The executive branch of the government also includes the attorney general, the auditor, and the treasurer.

LEGISLATIVE BRANCH

The legislative branch is responsible for making laws about things that are important to the people of Utah. For example, laws may be made to protect Utah's environment and wildlife, or to set aside money for projects such as repairing highways and creating public parks. The legislative branch also sets the state budget. The budget tells the legislative branch how much money the government has, and how much the state can spend.

The members of Utah's legislative branch are divided into two groups. They are the house of representatives and the senate. The senate has 29 members; one senator represents each of Utah's 29 counties. Each senator serves a four-year term. The house of representatives has 75 members who serve their districts for two years.

Senators and representatives are elected by the people during state elections. Citizens vote for representatives who feel the same as they do about important issues. In this way, everyone who votes has a say in how the state is being run.

JUDICIAL BRANCH

The judicial branch interprets, or explains, state law. It also decides on the punishment for people who break the laws. The judicial branch is made up of seven judicial districts. Each district has a judge who serves for six years. A judge's job is to make sure that people are treated fairly, and that each side of a case is heard in his or her courtroom.

WHO'S WHO IN UTAH?

George Sutherland (1862–1942) was born in England and raised in Utah County. He joined the first Utah house of representatives, and later became a United States senator. In 1922, Justice Sutherland became a United States Supreme Court justice, the only one from Utah.

UTAH STATE GOVERNMENT

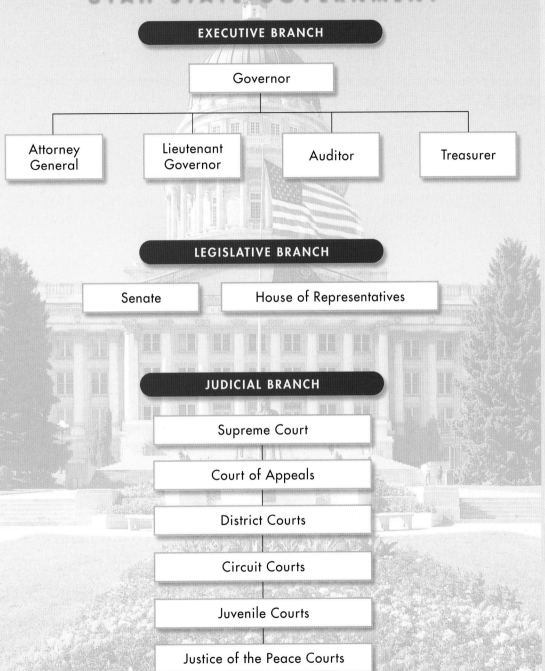

EXECUTIVE BRANCH

Governor

Attorney General

Lieutenant Governor

Auditor

Treasurer

LEGISLATIVE BRANCH

Senate

House of Representatives

JUDICIAL BRANCH

Supreme Court

Court of Appeals

District Courts

Circuit Courts

Juvenile Courts

Justice of the Peace Courts

UTAH GOVERNORS

Name	Term	Name	Term
Heber M. Wells	1896–1905	Joseph B. Lee	1949–1957
John C. Cutler	1905–1909	George D. Clyde	1957–1965
William Spry	1909–1917	Calvin L. Rampton	1965–1977
Simon Bamberger	1917–1921	Scott M. Matheson	1977–1985
Charles R. Mabey	1921–1925	Norman H. Bangerter	1985–1993
George H. Dern	1925-1933	Michael O. Leavitt	1993–2003
Henry H. Blood	1933–1941	Olene S. Walker	2003–2005
Herbert B. Maw	1941–1949	Jon M. Huntsman, Jr.	2005–

There are several types of courts in the judicial branch. Each court hears different kinds of cases. For example, juvenile courts hear cases in which young people (juveniles), have broken the law. Other courts include the court of appeals, district court, circuit courts, and justice of the peace courts. Utah's most important court is the state supreme court. Five justices (judges) serve ten-year terms on the supreme court.

TAKE A TOUR OF SALT LAKE CITY

When the first pioneers entered the Salt Lake Valley in the mid-1800s, the ground was sandy and dry. There were no buildings or streets. Today, Salt Lake Valley has changed beyond recognition. There are buildings everywhere, and more than 181,743 people live in Salt Lake City.

The streets of Salt Lake City were designed by Brigham Young, the city's founding father. The streets are laid out in a grid-like pattern around Temple Square. It is difficult to get lost in Salt Lake City because each street is numbered and has a compass direction, running north, south, east, or west.

Salt Lake City shines at night. The Salt Palace Convention Center and West Temple Street are shown here.

At 80 feet (24 m) wide, the streets are much broader than those in most cities. Brigham Young made the streets wide so that oxen-teams and heavy wagons could turn easily. There are no oxen-teams on Salt Lake City's streets now, except in July, when the state celebrates Pioneer Day with historic pageants and parades. Today, the streets are filled with cars and buses. Old-fashioned trolleys carry tourists to Temple Square and other downtown areas.

Temple Square is home to the Mormon Temple. The Mormons began building their Temple in 1853. They finished it 40 years later, in 1893. The Temple has six towers and spires. The center spire supports a 12 1/2-foot (3.8-m) gold statue of Angel Moroni, an ancient prophet. The Temple's walls are made of Utah granite and are 9 feet (2.7 m) thick at the base. The granite blocks had to be carted almost 25 miles (40 km) to the capital. Only members of the Mormon church are allowed inside the Temple.

Not far from the Temple is the Mormon Tabernacle, home of the world-famous

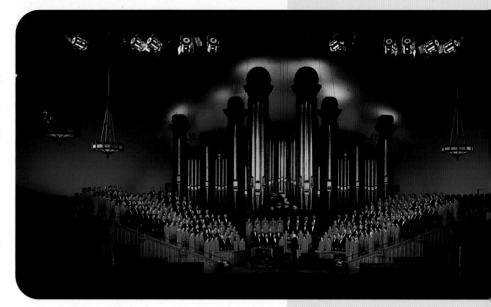

Mormon Tabernacle Choir. The choir has more than 300 members and has won many awards. The Tabernacle itself seats 6,500 people. Its beautiful pipe-organ is enormous, with 206 pipes.

You can't miss the copper dome and granite walls of the state capitol, which sits grandly on Capitol Hill above Senate Street. Most of the stone used to build the capitol was quarried in Utah. The stars and stripes of the United States flag and Utah's own blue-and-gold state flag flutter proudly in the wind in front of the capitol. You can tour the inside of the building to see the governor's office, the state legislature, and the supreme court in action.

A short distance away on North Main Street is the Pioneer Memorial Museum. There you can see dolls and toys that once belonged to the children of Utah's first pioneers. If you want to know more about Utah's history, visit Old Deseret Historical Village in Salt Lake's City's "This is the Place" State Park. Old Deseret is a living historic village. Actors and actresses are dressed in the costume of the first Mormon pioneers. The settlers' everyday lives will come to life, right before your eyes.

The Children's Museum of Utah is the next stop on our tour. At this exciting museum, you can discover for yourself how it feels to fly a jet, or try other fun hands-on scientific exhibits that are designed with children in mind.

The Mormon Tabernacle choir has performed in many countries.

(Opposite)
The Mormon Temple is open to faithful church members only.

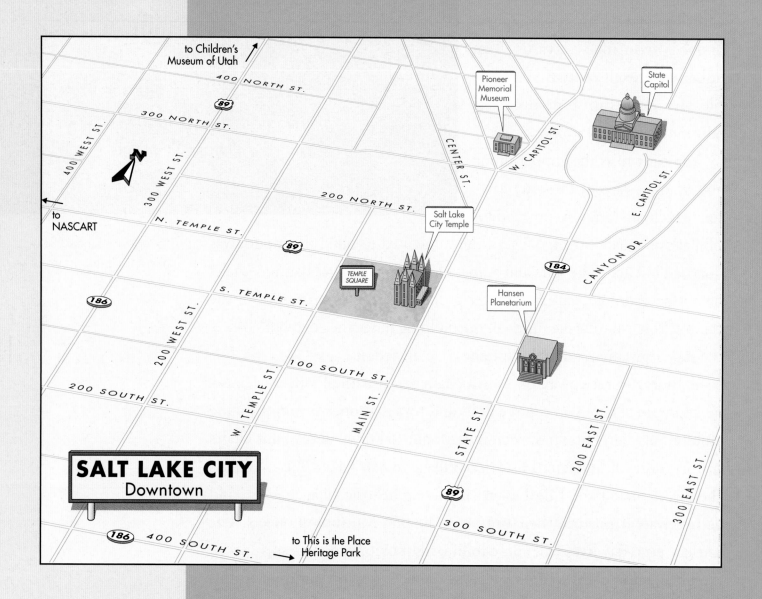

to Children's
Museum of Utah

400 NORTH ST.

300 NORTH ST.

89

400 WEST ST.

300 WEST ST.

to
NASCART

N. TEMPLE ST.

89

200 NORTH ST.

CENTER ST.

Pioneer
Memorial
Museum

State
Capitol

W. CAPITOL ST.

E. CAPITOL ST.

CANYON DR.

Salt Lake
City Temple

184

186

S. TEMPLE ST.

TEMPLE
SQUARE

Hansen
Planetarium

200 WEST ST.

W. TEMPLE ST.

100 SOUTH ST.

MAIN ST.

STATE ST.

200 EAST ST.

300 EAST ST.

200 SOUTH ST.

SALT LAKE CITY
Downtown

89

186

400 SOUTH ST.

to This is the Place
Heritage Park

300 SOUTH ST.

The Pioneer Museum features exhibits about the earliest settlers in Utah.

If astronomy is your idea of fun, then the Hansen Planetarium and Science Museum is definitely the place to do some stargazing. Check out the night sky through a state-of-the-art telescope. You might even discover a brand new star! Or take in a laser or star show. With new shows every month, there's always something exciting to see at the Hansen Planetarium.

You might not be old enough to drive, but you can still make a pit stop at Salt Lake's NASCART. This speedway has 2,000 feet (610 m) of indoor racetrack. It's the next best thing to getting the checkered flag!

There are so many fun things to do and see in Salt Lake City. Plan on taking more than just one day to tour Utah's beautiful capital city. You won't want to miss a thing.

CHAPTER FIVE

THE PEOPLE AND PLACES OF UTAH

Utahns celebrate their history by retracing the Mormon pioneer trail every July.

With a population of 2,233,169 residents, Utah has the 34th largest population in the United States. Almost 9 of every 10 people in Utah are of European descent. Most of their ancestors came from England, and the rest from other European countries. Just under 2 of every 100 people are Asian, 9 in every 100 have Hispanic origins, and less than 1 person in every 100 is African-American. Although they were the area's first inhabitants, fewer than 2 in every 100 people in Utah today are Native American. Most of Utah's 32,000 Native Americans live on the White Mesa Reservation near Bluff, or the Uintah-Ouray Indian Reservation near Fort Duchesne.

Although Utah is not the largest state, it has the second highest birthrate in the country, and the second lowest number of deaths. One reason why the state has such a healthy population might be that just over half of the state's residents are members of the LDS, or Mormon, church. Church members are encouraged to have big families. They also live a healthful lifestyle, and are not allowed to drink alcohol, consume caffeine, or smoke tobacco.

Many Mormons faithfully attend Sunday church services.

NATIVE AMERICANS

The Native Americans in Utah, as in other states, have struggled throughout history. By 1930, they had lost four-fifths of their tribal land. In 1948, the government started the Relocation Program. This program was intended to help Native Americans find well-paying jobs in the cities. However, most Native Americans did not like living or working in the city, and the project failed. Native American dreams of tribal government also ended.

Since 1909, several Native American groups have filed claims against the United States government for breaking its promises to Native Americans in the 1800s. These claims have resulted in cash settlements for the Ute, who received more than $3,500,000 from the government. In 1962, $47,700,000 was given to the Northern Ute peoples. The Southern Paiute and the Goshute have also received several million dollars. This money is used to improve the lives of Native Americans through creating educational programs, jobs, businesses, and other projects.

An organization called the Circle of Wellness was started by tribal members to keep Native American traditions and cultures alive. This organization has also started several companies. Now, Native Americans who do not want to leave the reservation are still able to find well-paying jobs in technology fields. In November 2001, hundreds of miles of high-speed optical cable were laid through the Uintah-Ouray Reservation. A new company called Uintah River Technology (URT) now provides high-tech jobs for Utah's Native Americans. The company is owned and operated by Native Americans. Dozens of tribal members now compete for well-paid jobs with URT.

Native American culture has not been lost since the Utes' entry into the world of high technology. Native American powwows, or dance festivals, are still held on reservation land. Native American dancers perform in traditional costume to celebrate their culture.

A family grooms a sheep in preparation for the Utah state fair.

WORKING IN UTAH

Since World War II, more Utahns have worked for the United States government than for any other employer. Today, the government employs about 24,165 civil service employees at Hill Air Force Base, the Tooele Army Depot, and the IRS Western Center.

A hundred years ago, agriculture was one of the state's biggest industries. Today, barley, hay, corn, and wheat are grown in Utah. Livestock and poultry farms produce eggs, chickens, pigs, sheep, and cattle.

Most Utahns work in service industries. Jobs in the service industry include salesclerks who ring up your groceries in the store, nurses who care for the sick, janitors who clean the schools, or bank tellers who cash your checks. Tourism is also part of the service industry. Tourism is the business of providing food, shelter, and entertainment for visitors. The $3.7 billion tourist industry is the fastest-growing industry in the state. The 2002 Winter Olympic Games, which were held in Salt Lake City, provided thousands of jobs for state residents, including security guards, janitors, dancers, and more.

Factories and industries along the Wasatch Front also provide jobs for many Utahns. They produce a huge variety of items such as medical instruments, automobile parts, computer components, and machinery. Other major Utah industries are printing and publishing, wood and paper products, and food processing.

Timber is also important to the state's economy. In 2000, 105 million board feet of timber, including pine and aspen, was taken from the Wasatch Front's mountain forests. The logging crews and sawmills that process the timber provide jobs for Utah's population.

The mining of non-fuel minerals, such as sand and gravel, is less important to the state's economy than it was in the past. However, copper, gold, magnesium metal, and Portland cement are still mined in the state.

Utah's successful movie and television industry has also created jobs for Utahns. This industry has grown quickly since the 1960s, thanks to motion picture actor and director Robert Redford. Every year, Redford holds the Sundance Film Festival in Park City. The film

Flags, tourists, and automobiles crowd the streets of Park City during the Sundance Film Festival.

festival encourages movie directors to film in Utah. Directors hire local workers for their production crews.

TAKE A TOUR OF UTAH

Northern Utah

Utah's largest cities, including the capital, Salt Lake City, are concentrated in the northern part of the state. In addition to being the center of state government, Salt Lake City is home to the Utah Jazz basketball team, the Ballet West Dance company, the Utah Opera, and the Utah Symphony. Not far from Salt Lake City is the Bonneville Salt Flats. The sparkling white salt beds of the Bonneville Speedway seem endless! Since the late 1800s, they have been used as a racetrack.

Leaving the Salt Lake area, head north to Ogden, population 77,226. Ogden was named after Peter Skene Ogden, a mountain man.

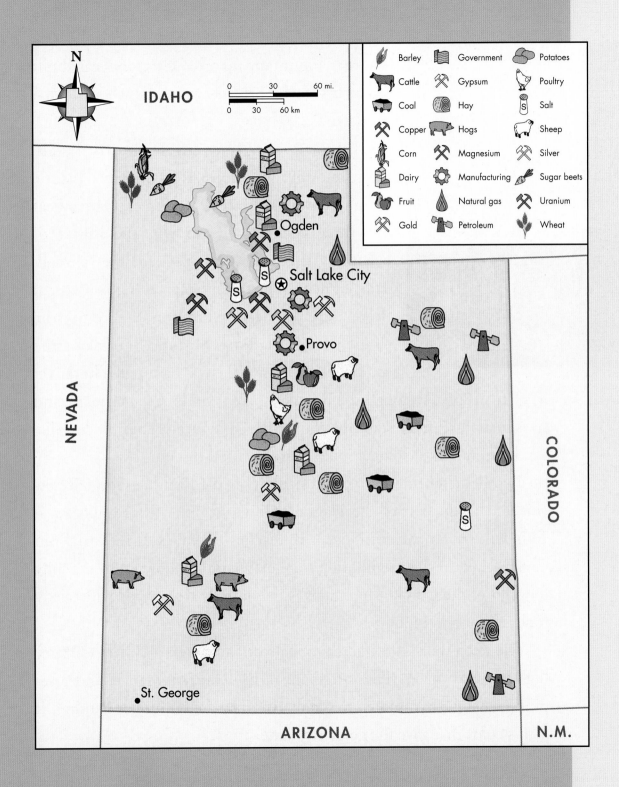

The Golden Spike National Historic Site reenacts the famous 1869 ceremony each year.

Another mountain man, Miles Goodyear, built Utah's first fort, Fort Buenaventura, where Ogden now stands.

Historic 25th Street, with its theaters, restaurants, and antique shops, is in Ogden. Historic Union Station is also on 25th Street. Ogden beat out three other towns to win the honor of becoming the central junction for the railroad. This earned Utah the nickname "Crossroads of the West." At nearby Promontory Point, the Golden Spike National Historic Site marks the spot where the last spike was hammered home on May 10, 1869. Although the original spike is no longer in the ground (it is in a museum at Stanford University), a replica of the golden spike can be seen at the Golden Spike Historic Site Museum.

Two hours northeast of Salt Lake City is the Flaming Gorge Reservoir and Dam, part of the Flaming Gorge National Recreation Area. This wilderness and artificial lake reaches 91 miles (146 km) from Green River, in the neighboring state of Wyoming, down into the hilly foothills of the Uintah Mountains. The foothills are covered with shady forests of fir and piñon trees.

The steep walls of the gorge, or canyon, are over 1,000 feet (305 m) high in many places. They are made of brilliant red, orange, and rose-pink sandstone and sometimes look as if they are on fire, or flaming. It is this color that gave the gorge its name.

Next, head south to Dinosaur National Monument. Its rocky landscape looks like the surface of the moon. You might spot petroglyphs (drawings carved into the rock) that were done by Utah's Paleo-Indians. One hundred years ago, this area was the hideout of Utah's most famous bad guy, Butch Cassidy, and his train-robbing "Hole in the Wall" gang.

Visitors examine a petroglyph at Dinosaur National Monument.

Thousands of dinosaur remains have been unearthed in this area. Most were found along a prehistoric riverbed that is now surrounded by glass. The result is a living museum, where visitors can watch paleonotologists search for fossils. More than 12,000 dinosaur bones and fossils have been found there.

After our visit to Dinosaur National Monument, head west to Vernal. The Utah Field House of Natural History has some great dinosaur exhibits, including the full-size skeleton of a diplocodous and a model of a tyrannosaurus rex.

Not far from Vernal is the Uintah-Ouray Indian Reservation, which stretches south from the foothills of the Uinta Mountains, near Fort Duchesne, and covers more than four million acres. Every summer,

WHO'S WHO IN UTAH?

Butch Cassidy (1866–1909), whose real name was Robert LeRoy Parker, was born near Beaver City, Utah. Cassidy and his partner, the Sundance Kid, were train robbers in the 1800s. Some say Cassidy was killed in a shootout in South America. The date of his death is in dispute.

This recipe will take you on a dinosaur "dig" that is nothing like the one at Utah's Dinosaur National Monument. When you are finished, you will have a delicious chocolate dessert for yourself and three hungry friends!

DINOSAUR DIG DESSERT

8 scoops of chocolate ice cream
4 chocolate brownies, cut in half horizontally
8 Oreo® cookies, crumbled (put cookies in a plastic
    bag and crush)
Assorted gummi candies, especially gummi dinosaurs,
    gummi worms, and so on. Allow 4–6 for each person.

1. Let chocolate ice cream soften slightly at room temperature (about ten minutes).
2. Place 1/2 brownie at the bottom of each of four dessert bowls.
3. Spoon one scoop of softened ice cream over each brownie. Spread ice cream evenly, using the back of a metal spoon dipped in warm tap water.
4. Sprinkle gummi dinosaurs over the ice cream layer. Press gummis firmly into the chocolate ice cream.
5. Place second 1/2 of brownie on top of gummi dinosaurs.
6. Spread another layer of ice cream over brownie.
7. Sprinkle ice cream with crushed Oreo® cookies.
8. Place desserts in freezer until ice cream has set again (about 20 minutes).
9. Use your spoon to dig deep. Eat your way through Oreo®"dirt" and layers of brownie "rock" to unearth dinosaur fossils. Enjoy your Dinosaur Dig Dessert!

Native American communities hold powwows there. Several tribes get together to celebrate Native American foods, dances, crafts, and other customs.

Next, try rafting down the Green River. For a little while, pretend that it's 1869, and that we're joining explorer John Wesley Powell and his ten companions on their journey down the Green and Colorado Rivers. As we ride the foaming water in our kayak, tall canyon walls rise sharply on either side of the river. The water all around us flows so fast, it is white with foam. The kayak bucks like a wild mustang, then the racing river sweeps us into unknown territory. The speed of our thrilling ride takes our breath away!

Central Utah

The Wasatch Mountain Range is our next stop. The first thing you'll notice is that the air is crisp and cool, and that the mountains are

The Green River is a popular place for boating, rafting, and canoeing.

65

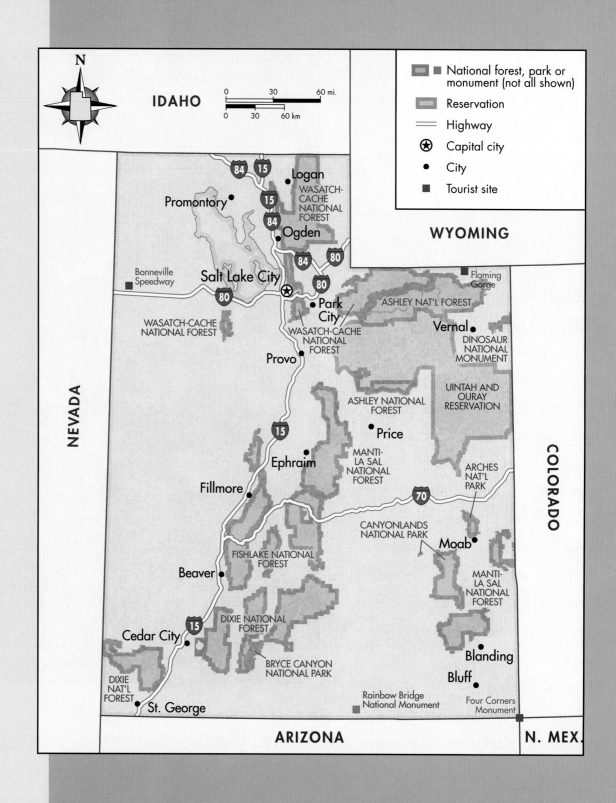

N

IDAHO

0 30 60 mi.
0 30 60 km

National forest, park or monument (not all shown)

Reservation

Highway

Capital city

City

Tourist site

WYOMING

84 15

Logan

WASATCH-CACHE NATIONAL FOREST

15

Promontory

84

Ogden

84 80

Bonneville Speedway

Flaming Gorge

ASHLEY NAT'L FOREST

Salt Lake City

80

80

Park City

WASATCH-CACHE NATIONAL FOREST

Vernal

DINOSAUR NATIONAL MONUMENT

WASATCH-CACHE NATIONAL FOREST

Provo

UINTAH AND OURAY RESERVATION

NEVADA

ASHLEY NATIONAL FOREST

15

Price

Ephraim

MANTI-LA SAL NATIONAL FOREST

ARCHES NAT'L PARK

70

Fillmore

CANYONLANDS NATIONAL PARK

Moab

COLORADO

FISHLAKE NATIONAL FOREST

MANTI-LA SAL NATIONAL FOREST

Beaver

DIXIE NATIONAL FOREST

15

Cedar City

Blanding

BRYCE CANYON NATIONAL PARK

Bluff

DIXIE NAT'L FOREST

Rainbow Bridge National Monument

Four Corners Monument

St. George

ARIZONA

N. MEX.

66

Students walk across the main plaza of Brigham Young University.

capped with powdery snow. At these elevations, there are cold, clear lakes jumping with cutthroat trout, the state fish. There are also shady pine forests of blue spruce trees. You might snowboard down the mountain slopes, or enjoy a hike through the wilderness.

Provo is the second largest city on the Wasatch Front. It is home to Brigham Young University, founded in 1875 as Brigham Young Academy. Today, more than 30,000 students attend the University.

Farther south, the old Mormon town of Moab was built in 1870. It is the best place to stay while you explore Canyonlands and Arches National Park. Moab was a mining town in the 1950s, but the mines are closed now. Today, Moab is popular with hikers, off-roaders, and river-runners. Movie producers and stuntmen also visit Moab. In fact, the Hollywood Stuntman's Hall of Fame is located there.

Southern Utah

Blanding, in southeastern Utah, is home of the mysterious Anasazi ruins. Traces of Utah's ancient ones are all over this area. The lands of the Navajo Nation lie to the southeast, reaching deep into Arizona and New Mexico. Farther south, near Bluff, is Four Corners, the only place

Visitors observe Four Corners monument from two different states.

in the United States where four states touch at one point. It is on land belonging to the Navajo Nation.

From Bluff, drive southwest for several hours. Then take a boat out to Rainbow Bridge, an enormous natural bridge of red rock. It stands on the shore of Lake Powell. The lake is now a beautiful recreation area. With close to 2,000 miles (3,219 km) of lakeshore, Lake Powell is a great place for a family vacation. Visitors can enjoy boating, hiking, camping, and sightseeing.

From Lake Powell head west to St. George, population 49,663. St. George is where Brigham Young had his second home. Nearby, in the City of the Gods scenic area, is the Tuacahn Center for the Performing Arts. Broadway shows, and concerts are performed there in a beautiful outdoor theater beneath the stars. For more theater opportunities, visit Cedar City, home of the award-winning Utah Shakespearean Festival. Every summer, more than 150,000 people visit the Festival's two theaters to watch plays written by Shakespeare and other well-known playwrights.

Whether you enjoy kayaking down the Colorado River, exploring Anasazi ruins, taking in a Jazz basketball game, or snowboarding, there's always something exciting and different to do in Utah!

UTAH ALMANAC

Statehood date and number: January 4, 1896/45th

State seal: The state seal shows an eagle with its wings spread. Below the eagle is a beehive. On either side of the beehive are white sego lilies. Around the beehive, there are banners with the stars and stripes of the United States. Below the bee-hive is the date that the state was first settled, 1847. Below this is the date that Utah was granted statehood, 1896. Adopted in 1896.

State flag: Utah's state flag has a medium-blue background bordered with gold. The state seal is shown at the center. Adopted in 1913.

Geographic center: Sanpete County, north of Manti

Total area/rank: 84,899 square miles (219,887 sq km)/11th

Borders: Idaho, Nevada, Arizona, New Mexico, Colorado, and Wyoming

Latitude and longitude: Utah is located approximately between 40° 45' 39'' and 111° 53' 25''

Highest/lowest elevation: 13,528 feet (4,123 m) at King's Peak in Duchesne County/2,000 feet (610 m) above sea level, at Beaverdam Creek in Washington County

Hottest/coldest temperature: 117°F (47°C) on July 5, 1985 at St. George/–69°F (–56°C) on February 1, 1985 at Peter's Sink

Land area/rank: 82,144 square miles (212,752 sq km)/12th

Inland water area/rank: 2,755 square miles (7,135 sq km)/7th

Population (2000 census)/rank: 2,233,169/34th

Population of major cities:

Salt Lake City: 181,743

Provo: 105,166

Ogden: 77,226

Saint George: 49,663

Logan: 42,670

Origin of state name: *Utah* is a Native American word meaning "people of the mountain"

State capital: Salt Lake City

Counties: 29

State government: 29 senators, 75 representatives

Major rivers/lakes: Colorado River, Green River/Great Salt Lake, Utah Lake, Lake Powell

Farming products: Hay, corn, wheat, barley, fruits

Livestock: Cattle, sheep, hogs, chickens

Manufactured products: Medical instruments, electronic parts, food products, steel, copper

Mining products: Gold, silver, copper, radium, uranium, coal

Bird: California seagull

Fish: Bonneville cutthroat trout

Flower: Sego lily

Folk dance: Square dance

Fossil: Allosaurus

Fruit: Cherry

Gem: Topaz

Grass: Indian ricegrass

Insect: Honey bee

Mammal: Elk

Mineral: Copper

Nickname: The Beehive State

Rock: Coal

Song: "Utah, We Love Thee!" by Evan Stephens

Tree: Blue spruce

Wildlife: Elk, mule-deer, bobcat, cougar, beaver, fox, rattlesnake, lizard

TIMELINE

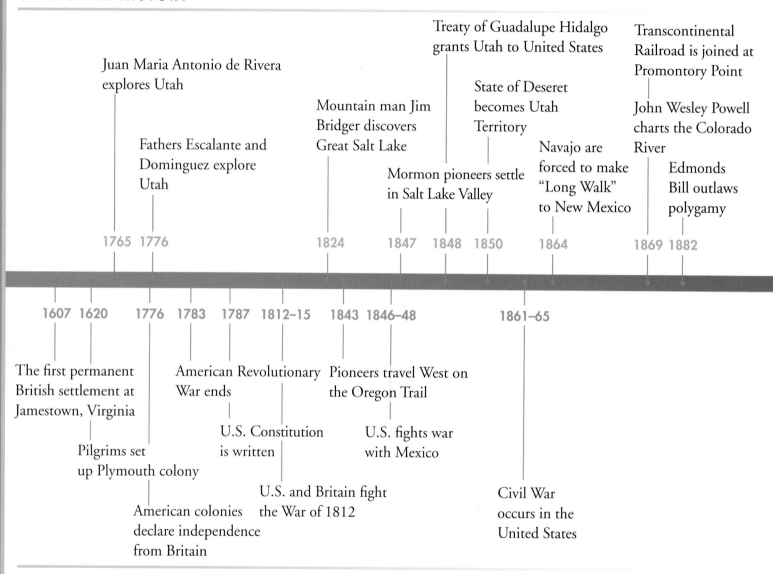

UTAH STATE HISTORY

Juan Maria Antonio de Rivera explores Utah

Fathers Escalante and Dominguez explore Utah

Mountain man Jim Bridger discovers Great Salt Lake

Mormon pioneers settle in Salt Lake Valley

Treaty of Guadalupe Hidalgo grants Utah to United States

State of Deseret becomes Utah Territory

Navajo are forced to make "Long Walk" to New Mexico

Transcontinental Railroad is joined at Promontory Point

John Wesley Powell charts the Colorado River

Edmonds Bill outlaws polygamy

1765 1776 — 1824 — 1847 1848 1850 — 1864 — 1869 1882

1607 1620 — 1776 1783 1787 1812–15 — 1843 1846–48 — 1861–65

The first permanent British settlement at Jamestown, Virginia

Pilgrims set up Plymouth colony

American colonies declare independence from Britain

American Revolutionary War ends

U.S. Constitution is written

U.S. and Britain fight the War of 1812

Pioneers travel West on the Oregon Trail

U.S. fights war with Mexico

Civil War occurs in the United States

UNITED STATES HISTORY

72

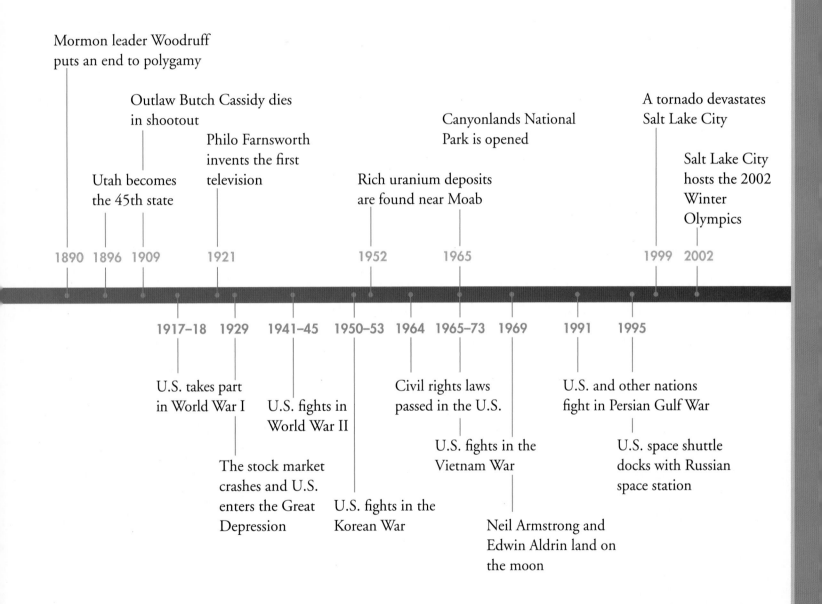

Mormon leader Woodruff
puts an end to polygamy

Outlaw Butch Cassidy dies
in shootout

Philo Farnsworth
invents the first
television

Canyonlands National
Park is opened

A tornado devastates
Salt Lake City

Salt Lake City
hosts the 2002
Winter
Olympics

Utah becomes
the 45th state

Rich uranium deposits
are found near Moab

1890 1896 1909   1921   1952   1965   1999 2002

1917–18 1929   1941–45   1950–53 1964 1965–73 1969   1991   1995

U.S. takes part
in World War I

U.S. fights in
World War II

Civil rights laws
passed in the U.S.

U.S. and other nations
fight in Persian Gulf War

U.S. fights in the
Vietnam War

U.S. space shuttle
docks with Russian
space station

The stock market
crashes and U.S.
enters the Great
Depression

U.S. fights in the
Korean War

Neil Armstrong and
Edwin Aldrin land on
the moon

GALLERY OF FAMOUS UTAHNS

Shawn Bradley

(1972–)

At 7' 6'' tall, NBA great Shawn Bradley played center for the Dallas Mavericks. He played basketball for Brigham Young University and lived in Castle Valley.

John Moses Browning

(1855–1926)

Gunsmith and inventor. Founder of Browning Brothers Company, producer of innovative firearms used in World War I. Born in Ogden.

Philo Farnsworth

(1906–1971)

An electrical engineer who invented the television when he was just 21 years old. Born near Beaver City.

Debbi Fields

(1956–)

Founded Mrs. Fields Cookies, a chain of cookie and baked-goods stores, at the age of 21. Lived in Salt Lake City.

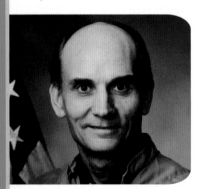

Jake Garn

(1932–)

The first United States congressman to travel in space. He served as a payload specialist aboard the space shuttle *Discovery* in 1985. Born in Richfield.

Daniel Jackling

(1869–1956)

The "father of Utah copper mining." He helped found the Utah Copper Company and began mining in Bingham Canyon. Lived in Mercer and Salt Lake City.

J. Willard Marriott

(1900–1985)

Founder of Marriott Hotel, one of the most successful hotel chains in the world. Born in Marriott Settlement, Utah, and graduated from the University of Utah.

Donny and Marie Osmond

(1957–), (1959–)

Well-known brother and sister team of entertainers. Born in Ogden.

Robert Redford

(1937–)

Famous American actor and director. Founder of the Sundance Institute, an organization that encourages and assists young, independent filmmakers. Born in California and lives part time in Provo Canyon.

Mahonri Young

(1877–1957)

American sculptor, painter, and etcher. Creator of the Sea Gull Monument in Salt Lake City. Born in Salt Lake City.

GLOSSARY

adobe: a type of clay or mud that hardens as it dries

constitution: a set of rules about how a state or country should be governed

erosion: the gradual wearing away of land by wind, water, or ice

evaporate: when water is dispersed throughout the air in the form of very small drops

fossils: the hardened remains of animals or plants from long ago

geologist: a scientist who studies the earth's crust

innovative: something newly introduced

mesa: a high, steep-sided rock plateau

mission: a place where European priests taught Native Americans about the Christian religion

nomads: wanderers; people who travel from place to place

paleontologist: a scientist who studies ancient forms of life

plateau: a flat, level area of land

polygamy: having more than one wife or husband at the same time

prehistoric: before history was written down

FOR MORE INFORMATION

Web sites

Utah State Historical Society

http://history.utah.gov
Check out the History for Kids page for interesting Utah facts and history.

Enchanted Learning; All About Dinosaurs

http://www.enchantedlearning.com/subjects/dinosaurs/dinos/Utahraptor.shtml
Learn more about the utahraptor.

The Official Website for Utah Government

http://www.utah.gov/
Provides links to information about Utah government, places to visit, and more.

State of Utah Resource Web (SURWEB)

http://www.surweb.org/
Educational site providing information, pictures, and trivia about Utah and other parts of the United States.

Books

Glass, Andrew. *Mountain Men: True Grit and Tall Tales.* New York, NY: Delacorte Press, 2001.

Lessem, Don. *All the Dirt on Dinosaurs.* New York, NY: Tor Books, 2001.

Simon, Charnan. *Brigham Young: Mormon and Pioneer (Community Builders).* Danbury, CT: Children's Press, 1999.

Addresses

Office of the Governor
State Capitol Complex
East Office Building Suite E220
P.O. Box 142220
Salt Lake City, UT 84114-2220

Utah Travel Council
Utah Office of Tourism
Council Hall / Capitol Hill
300 N. State Street
Salt Lake City, UT 84114

Utah State Historical Society
300 South Rio Grande
Salt Lake City, UT 84101-1143

INDEX

ABOUT THE AUTHOR

P. J. Neri is the author of *Hawai'i Chillers*, a spooky fiction series for children. She has also written more than 27 books for adults, which are published worldwide. Born in Suffolk, England, P. J. lives in Hawaii with her husband and dogs, Heidi and Holly. She enjoys traveling, music, painting, and reading.

Photographs © 2009: AP Images: 60 (Steve C. Wilson), 74 left; Bob Clemenz Photography: 62; Church of Latter Day Saints: 53; Corbis Images: 46 (Peter Andrews/Reuters NewMedia Inc.), 18 (Lester V. Bergman), 48 (Bettmann), 63 bottom (Jonathan Blair), 67 (Phil Schermeister), 45 (UPI), 35; Dave G. Houser/HouserStock, Inc.: 55, 63 top (Jan Butchofsky), 17, 52; Dembinsky Photo Assoc./Scott T. Smith: 11, 51; Dietrich Stock Photo: 44; Gene Ahrens: 47, 49 background; Getty Images: 56 (J. Allred), 37 (Archive Photos), 68 (David Ball/Stone), 74 right (Jim Bourg/Reuters/Archive Photos), 4 (David Epperson/Stone), 39, 43 (Hulton Archive), 14 (George Lepp/Stone); Lieutenant Governor's Office, Salt Lake City, UT: 70 top; MapQuest.com, Inc.: 70 bottom; Nativestock.com/Marilyn "Angel" Wynn: 26; North Wind Picture Archives: 20 top, 25, 27, 28, 29, 31 top, 34, 36; Photo Researchers, NY: 3 right, 10 (Keith Kent/SPL), 70 top left (Rod Planck), 15 (Stephen Saks); Robert Holmes Photography/Dewitt Jones: 8, 23; Robertstock.com: 38 (Charles Phelps Cushing), 24 (P. Kresan), 3 left, 20 bottom (P. Royer), 65 (R. Walker); Stock Montage, Inc.: 22, 30, 31 bottom, 32, 41; Superstock, Inc.: 33; Tom Till Photography, Inc.: cover, 7, 16, 19; Unicorn Stock Photos/A Ramey/CPI: 57; Visuals Unlimited: 71 right (Gerald & Buff Corsi), 58 (Mark E. Gibson), 70 bottom left (W. Omerod).